OBJECTIONS *to* ELECTION ANSWERED

GREAT CHRISTIAN BOOKS
LINDENHURST, NEW YORK

OBJECTIONS

to

ELECTION

ANSWERED

HENRY A.
BOARDMAN

Great Christian Books

is an imprint of Rotolo Media

160 37th Street Lindenhurst, New York 11757

(631) 956-0998

Boardman, Henry Augustus, 1808 - 1880
Objections to Election: Answered / by Henry A. Boardman
p. cm.
A "A Great Christian Book" book
GREAT CHRISTIAN BOOKS an imprint of Rotolo Media
ISBN 978-1-61010-031-1
Recommended Dewey Decimal Classifications: 200, 202, 230, 234
Suggested Subject Headings:
1. Religion—Christianity & Christian theology—Salvation
2. Christianity—Doctrine—Election
I. Title

Book and cover design are by Michael Rotolo, www.michaelrotolo.com. This book is typeset in the Minion typeface by Adobe Inc. and is quality-manufactured on acid-free paper stock. To discuss the publication of your Christian manuscript or out-of-print book, please contact us.

Manufactured in the United States of America

– CONTENTS –

Philadelphia, Dec. 30, 1848

Rev. Henry A. Boardman, D.D.

Dear Sir,

The undersigned, members of the congregation under your pastoral care, listened with much interest to the Sermons recently preached by you, on what is popularly termed the subject of election. On reflection, it has seemed to us that so many of the views which the advocates of that time-honored and vital doctrine are called upon to discuss in private life, are there considered, that the publication of the discourses could not fail to produce extensive practical benefit. Permit us, therefore, to request that unless an objection to such a course shall present itself to your mind, you will furnish us with your manuscript for this purpose.

We are your attached friends,

Wm. A. Porter,
Chas. B. Penrose,
W. H. Dillingham,
John R. Vogdes,
Moses Johnson,
C. B. Jaudon,
A. W. Mitchell
Wm. Harris

BOARDMAN'S RESPONSE

Gentlemen,

The Sermons you have requested for publication, were prepared and preached under a strong conviction that the doctrine of election was by one large class of persons misunderstood, and by another grossly perverted. The popular conceptions of the doctrine are those which have been supplied by its adversaries; and the objections to which these are justly obnoxious, have been somewhat industriously employed to bring the doctrine itself into discredit, and even to discourage inquiry into its scriptural authority. From this cause, doubtless, the feeling has come to prevail, that 'the whole subject is one which had better be let alone; and that the pulpit should confine itself to topics .of a less mysterious and more practical nature. But surely "*all* scripture is profitable:" truth is in order to holiness: and if election be taught, and very prominently taught in the word of God, it is not only out duty to receive it, but the belief of it must tend legitimately to promote personal religion and real peace of mind. No one need fear as to the *tendency* of any doctrine of the Bible. It is when the sacred truths of revelation have been deformed and caricatured, that they exert an influence prejudicial to sound morality, or minister to the alarm of timid and doubting Christians. In no other way can we explain the state of feeling now so common respecting election—a doctrine so clearly and unequivocally taught in the Scriptures, that nearly all the Reformed Churches have embraced it in their Confessions, and the due "consideration of which (as the Church of England says in her Articles) is full of sweet, pleasant, and unspeakable comfort to godly persons."

It was with a view of removing misconceptions and vindicating the doctrine from the more specious of the common objections urged against it, that the following discourses were written. This, I hope, will be kept in mind by those into whose hands they may fall. Had my object been to discuss the doctrine itself, the whole framework of the argument would of course have been different, and the scriptural proofs of the doctrine would have been cited in due form.

I am gratified to learn by your polite note, that the Sermons have not, in your judgment, entirely failed of their mission; and in the hope that they may, by the blessing of God, be still further useful, I submit the manuscript to your disposal.

I remain, gentlemen, with great respect.

Your friend and pastor,
H. A. BOARDMAN.

Messrs.—
Wm. A. Porter, Charles B. Penrose,
Wm. H. Dillingham, John R. Vogdes,
Moses Johnson, Charles B. Jaudon.
A. W. Mitchell, M.D. Wm. Harris, M.D.

THE DOCTRINE OF ELECTION NOT DEROGATORY TO GOD

"According as he hath chosen us in him before the foundation of the world, that we should be holy and without blame before him in love; having predestinated us unto the adoption of children by Jesus Christ to himself, according to the good pleasure of his will, to the praise of the glory of his grace, wherein he hath made us accepted in the Beloved." —Ephesians 1:4-6

No doctrine of Christianity has more reason to complain of the treatment it has received, than the doctrine of Election. With many persons, the very name is an offence; and they will scarcely listen even to an exposition of those texts of Scripture in which the word occurs. It is associated in their minds with all that is unjust and vindictive: and the attempt to establish it by argument, disturbs their equanimity, if it does not even awaken their resentment. The unfairness of the course here hinted at, must be apparent to every candid inquirer after truth. The class of persons alluded to must surely be aware that our natural feelings constitute no fit standard for testing the truth of a doctrine. As in physical science manythings have been found to be true which were once universally discredited, so it may very well happen in theology, the first of all sciences, that many doctrines shall prove to have a solid foundation in the word of God, which are quite at variance with the common prepossessions and prejudices of men. This remark will apply to the doctrines of the Trinity, regeneration, justification, and possibly some others which are fundamental to the Christian scheme. Why may it not apply also to the doctrine of election? When we remember that the relation in which we stand to the Deity is that of apostates and condemned criminals, there is a palpable incongruity in the idea of leaving the credibility of *this* doctrine to be determined by the promptings of our own hearts, irrespective of the testimony of Scripture.

Another consideration which should abate the violence of opposition to this doctrine, is that it has not only been embraced and defended by many of the wisest and purest men in the best days of the Church, but is at this moment embodied in the creeds and confessions of the great mass of Protestant Christendom.* This is not said with a view

---

* As a single specimen, take the following from the XVIIth Article of the Church of England— "Predestination to life is the everlasting purpose of God, whereby (before the foundations of the world were laid,) he hath constantly decreed by his counsel, secret to us, to deliver from curse and damnation those whom he hath chosen in Christ out of mankind, and to bring them by Christ to everlasting salvation as vessels made to honor."

of sustaining by mere human authority, a doctrine which lacks higher support. But something is due to the opinions of a large and intelligent body of men on any subject; and the fact that the doctrine in question has been received by the Christian Church generally, must have great weight with every candid person in securing for it a respectful and thorough consideration before it is finally rejected.

These observations are designed to prepare the way for a brief examination of one of the popular objections to the doctrine of election, viz.: that it is derogatory to the Divine Character. It is often said that this doctrine, "instead of representing the Deity as the indulgent Father of his creatures, makes him a tyrant, who has created men merely to damn them, and who delights in witnessing their eternal sufferings."

This is a serious allegation, and if it can be sustained, the advocates of the doctrine must repudiate it with indignation. But let us see whether it does not proceed upon a total misconception of the doctrine; and whether the charge which is here preferred does not, in so far as it has any real weight, lie with equal, if not greater force, against the systems of those who reject it.

What, then, is the doctrine of election? I answer, in brief, it is this:—God has, from eternity, out of his mere good pleasure, chosen in Christ a certain definite portion of our lost race unto everlasting glory. The persons thus chosen, being fallen in Adam, have been redeemed by the Lord Jesus Christ: they are effectually called unto faith in Christ by his Spirit working in due season; and they are justified, adopted, sanctified, and kept by his power through faith unto salvation. The rest of mankind, God was pleased, according to the unsearchable counsel of his own will, to pass by and leave to the just consequences of their own sins.

Now it will be seen at once that the Deity was under no obligation to save a single individual of our race. If he was, there is no grace in redemption: the death of Christ was a debt due to us which he had no right to withhold; and those who enter heaven, may ascribe their salvation, not to the boundless mercy of God, but to their own merits. This point, however, need not be argued; since it is conceded by most professed believers in Christianity, Socinians and Pelagians excepted, with whom at present I do not contend, that the justice of God would have been unimpeached had he left our whole race to suffer the penal consequences of their rebellion. If then justice would have sanctioned the final condemnation of the whole race, where is the injustice of saving a part? If a thousand subjects are sentenced to die for engaging in a traitorous conspiracy against their Prince, is he to be charged with tyranny because he sees fit to extend his clemency to one half of them and pardon them? Would this afford any just ground of complaint to the remainder? Their sentence is not less righteous than it was before then* companions were liberated; nor is its severity enhanced. They suffer now precisely what they would have suffered without this display of the royal compassion to their fellows; and they and all men must see that there is no wrong done in inflicting upon them the penalty of the law. So also in the case before us. The decree of election, let it be remembered, *finds men sinners:* it has no agency in making them sinners. This is sometimes strangely overlooked. Language is frequently used in the discussion of this subject, which seems to imply that God has by a positive influence brought men into a state of guilt and misery, and that having done this, he refuses to extricate them from it. That he has, for wise and holy purposes not revealed to us, *permitted* our race to fall into sin, is most true. Why he has done so, is a question on which many volumes have been written, perhaps to little purpose. It is easy to see how the apostasy of mankind may be, in some particulars, overruled for good. The astonishing display of the Divine perfections, furnished by the work of redemption, and the height of glory to which the saints will be exalted hereafter, are among the great and beneficent results that have been educed from the awful catastrophe in which the race has been overwhelmed. And we infer from the nature of the moral government of God, and from some obscure intimations in the Scriptures, that the events which have occurred in our world will yet have an important influence upon every part of His wide empire. Still, after all our reasonings and conjectures, there is a mystery about the permission of evil which is inexplicable to us in our present imperfect state. It is an ocean we cannot fathom. That God foresaw all the consequences which were to follow the fall of Adam, that he knew it would involve millions of souls in everlasting misery, that he could have prevented it, had he seen fit to exert his power for that purpose, but that he actually permitted it to take place, are plain facts which must be admitted by every humble believer in Christianity.

Beyond the facts we cannot go. Happily we are not required to explain them. We receive them as facts, on the testimony of God: and although we cannot clear them up, we bow submissively to the teachings of the Spirit, and are satisfied that there is nothing in the Divine procedure in these transactions which is at all at variance with the glorious perfections of the Godhead.

Now the facts just stated are the same, what, ever views may be adopted respecting the application of the remedy which has been provided for the evils of the fall. Men may receive or reject the doctrine of election: the fact still remains, that our race have sinned, and are therefore under the wrath and curse of God. The lost condition of the race is a fact independent of election; a fact, therefore, which it devolves as much upon the impugners of that doctrine to explain, as upon its friends; and one which presses with equal weight upon their theories. We say, the race is in ruins; and they assent to it. We say, further, that God was not bound to provide a Savior for any portion of the race; and that to assert the contrary, is to maintain the principle that whenever a subject commits a crime, his sovereign is under obligation, at whatever expense or sacrifice, to proffer him a pardon. Contemplating the race in its guilt and misery, God was pleased to determine that he would rescue a certain number from the doom which all had incurred. Was this injustice? Was this tyranny? Are similar acts on the part of earthly kings ever branded with these epithets? Are they not rather applauded as acts of singular lenity and kindness? And if an example were to occur of a prince who should pardon part of a band of conspirators, even when, from reasons of state, he must, in order to do it, make a sacrifice equivalent to that of surrendering an only son to an ignominious death; what would be thought of men who should contend that this sublime and affecting transaction was only an evidence of his cruelty!—who, instead of extolling his generosity and benevolence in pardoning at such a cost a portion of the traitors, should only cavil because he had not pardoned the whole! This illustration appears to me to present in its true light the objection to the doctrine of election which we are considering. So far from being an evidence of cruelty, the decree of election is the offspring of pure, ineffable, and eternal love. Sovereign love, I grant it is, as everything else is which pertains to the Deity. But still it is love. If there be any love in the gift of God's only-begotten Son to die for us, if there be any love in the sufferings and death of Christ, if there be any love in rescuing millions and millions of souls from hell, and raising them to everlasting glory and felicity, then is election the fruit of love and not of wrath. For election lies at the foundation of redemption and all its beneficent results: "for whom he did predestinate," (that is, whom he chose in Christ Jesus before the foundation of the world,) "them he also called, and whom he called, them he also justified, and whom he justified, them he also glorified." So far should we be from repudiating this precious doctrine, or investing it with terror, that we ought to cling to it as the ground of our hopes, and fly to it in seasons of trial as the anchor of our souls.

Here, in so far as the justice of God is concerned, the discussion, it is believed, might be safely closed. But this doctrine is chained with presenting the Divine character in a repulsive aspect, in other particulars, and I must detain you with a further consideration of the subject.

It is contended that we place needless limitations to the mercy of God, in representing him as restricting his love to a part of the race.— "Since he is infinitely good (it is argued,) he must delight in the happiness of *all* his creatures. How then can he select a portion of them as the objects of his special regard, and leave the rest to perish? Surely it is more honorable to the Deity to suppose that he makes no such discrimination among them as this doctrine implies, but loves them all with an equal love, and employs, in all instances, the same means for their salvation."

These sentiments commend themselves, it is readily granted, to the best feelings of our hearts, and they seem to present the character of God in a very amiable aspect. To sinful creatures mercy must always appear a more lovely attribute than justice; and it seems at first view to be highly honorable to the Creator, to represent him as extending the same compassion to each individual of our fallen race. But we are not, on a question of this kind, to take counsel of our own feelings. Our inquiry is not as to what God might have done, nor as to what we should have preferred his doing, but as to what he has done.

The objection affirms the goodness of God. On this point there can be no controversy: this attribute beams forth from the works of nature, and from the pages of revelation, with the splendor of a noon-tide sun. But the objection farther assumes that because God is good, he is bound, by the necessity of his nature, to do all the good he can to each one of his creatures. This inference is false in philosophy and in fact. It proceeds upon the notion that the possession of an attribute or faculty, involves necessarily the constant exercise of it, and that to its full extent. This is so palpably erroneous that the mere statement of it must be sufficient to show its absurdity. The perfections of Jehovah are, it is true, in one sense, infinite, but they must be limited by each other in their exercise; otherwise there would be a continual conflict in the Divine mind; and the Supreme Being, instead of enjoying ineffable happiness, would be miserable in himself and most inconsistent in his actions. As to the particular attribute under consideration, it should be remembered that goodness ceases to be goodness unless it is directed by wisdom. If we separate it from this, we degrade it to the level of a mere instinct, which, as it would operate without intelligence or design, so it could excite neither our respect nor our gratitude.

Observe, again, how irreconcilable with obvious and admitted facts, is the principle on which this objection is founded, viz.: the principle that because God is good, he is bound to *do all he can* to preserve his creatures from suffering and to make them individually happy. I say "individually happy," because both reason and Scripture require us to believe that he will seek the happiness of the intelligent universe *as a whole*, in that way which may most effectually promote his own glory.

However agreeable it might be to our conceptions of the Divine character to suppose that he would not permit a single one of his creatures to suffer, if he could prevent it, we perceive at a glance that this sentiment is discountenanced by the whole history of his dispensations towards our race. The apostasy of our first parents, already adverted to, is an illustration in point. Could he not have prevented that, had he seen fit to do it? And after permitting it, might he not have arrested the consequences of it with the guilty pair themselves, without allowing the curse to be entailed upon the countless generations of their posterity? Look, too, at the varied evils under which mankind have been groaning ever since the fall. Look at the pains and sicknesses, the poverty and ignorance, the injustice and oppression, the vices and cruelties, with which the earth is scourged. Are not these things under God's control, and might he not remove them if he saw fit to do so?—Take another class of facts still more to our purpose in this argument, viz.: facts which show that he has exercised his sovereignty in *relieving* a part of the race from the effects of the apostasy. There was a wide difference in the characters even of Adam's two sons: one of them was, by a Divine influence, made a believer, the other was left an unbeliever; one was adopted as a child of God, the other remained a child of the devil. In the same sovereign manner, God became the friend and protector of Noah and his family, and destroyed all the other families of the earth with a flood. He revealed the true religion to Abraham and a portion of his descendants, and left the rest of the nations to idolatry and the terrible retribution he has denounced against it. Under the Christian dispensation he has given the gospel to some countries and withheld it from others, and in not a few instances he has withdrawn it from lands which once possessed it. Nay, he has distributed his favors among the inhabitants of the same land and within the same community, with the like inequality—some individuals being placed in situations highly favorable to their spiritual welfare, and others in circumstances so hostile to religion that their salvation would be little short of a miracle.

Now in reference to these and other similar facts, we are presented with a single alternative. We must either maintain that these events are not under the control of God, and that he could not alter them if he would, or we must admit that he does, for wise purposes, permit his creatures to suffer, and that he exercises his sovereignty in *making a difference* between them. The former branch of this alternative will not be taken by any one who has a proper veneration for the Deity; and I shall therefore waste no time in considering it. The only specious way in which the force of the latter part of it can be evaded, is this, viz.: by alleging that the difference which it is here asserted is made by Jehovah among his creatures, is a difference in their temporal circumstances merely, not in their spiritual and eternal state. It is obvious to remark in reply, that the principle involved is the same, whether the diversity created among them pertains to the present or the future life: if it would be incompatible with the Divine perfections to sanction it in the one case, it must be equally so in the other. But, waiving this, who does not see that the plea has no foundation in fact? It is not true that the diversified allotments which are assigned to our race in this world, are restricted in their influence to the present life. It is too manifest to admit of a question, that in appointing the temporal condition of men, with all its attendant circumstances, God does, to a great extent, decide their eternal destiny. There is, for example, a moral certainty that the individuals who are born in the heart of Asia or Africa, will perish in their sins, and go down with all idolaters to the lake which burneth with fire and brimstone. Can it be said that in so ordering events as to ensure their birth in the midst of pagan superstitions, the Creator has determined nothing in regard to their prospects for eternity? And as to Christian lands, does he determine nothing as to the future life in giving to some individuals, pious parents, a religious education, free access to all the means of grace, and a circle of friends whose example and counsels are adapted to lead them into the way of salvation; while others, the children of vicious parents, are left to grow up in ignorance of the God who made them, daily exposed to all the enticements of intemperance and debauchery, and without a single friend to admonish them of their danger and to care for their souls? Surely these familiar facts are sufficient to show, that while God is merciful and kind he claims the right to dispose of his creatures in that way which may best promote the great ends of his government; and none are permitted to 'stay his hand or say unto him, What doest thou?'

We need not, however, rest here. There are other facts which deserve the special attention of those who, from the most amiable motives, are so prompt in repelling as a slander upon the Almighty, the idea that he can elect one portion of our race to salvation and leave the rest to perish. How, on the principles assumed by these persons, is the providence of God *towards the angels* to be explained? Here there is no room for conjecture. It is a fact recorded by inspired men, that a part of the angelic throng have rebelled against God, and that he has sent them down to hell, to suffer eternal torment and despair. How is this to be reconciled to the divine goodness, by those who denounce the doctrine of election with so much vehemence, in its application to the human family? Was there no election here? If not, why are the holy angels called the "elect angels?" and why are they steadfast in holiness, while their fellows, once as glorious in purity and intelligence as they, are writhing under the vengeance of eternal fire? Is it said, that the lost spirits are only suffering the punishment due to their crimes? This is true: but the question still recurs, why were they *permitted* to rebel? Why did not the same hand which had previously held them up, and which still upholds their companions, defend them from that fatal temptation by which they were overcome, and for yielding to which they were hurled as lightning from heaven? I do not ask these questions expecting them to be answered. For setting aside the impious answer of those modem theologians who say that *God could not prevent their apostasy*; no solution of the mystery can be given: we can only resolve it, as all sincere and humble Christians are accustomed to do, into the sovereign pleasure of God, and say, "Even so, Father, for so it seemed good in thy sight." But the questions are designed to show that no argument can be drawn from the goodness of the Deity, to disprove the doctrine of election. We bring forward the acknowledged *fact*, that in the case of an order of creatures every way more exalted than our own, God has displayed his sovereignty in allowing some of them to fall, to rise no more, while he has confirmed the remainder in holiness and happiness. Inexplicable as this procedure appears to us, we do not allow it to affect in the least degree our notions of the Divine goodness. Our confidence in his rectitude, his benevolence, and his mercy, cannot be shaken even by the weeping and wailing which resound through the gloomy prison of those once pure and blessed beings. Why then should it be thought a thing incredible that the all-wise Creator should pursue a similar course towards ourselves? How can it be incompatible with his goodness to do with our race, as we know he has done with the angels? And with what reason can it be alleged that the decree of election makes Him a "tyrant," when applied to us, although it involves no impeachment of his justice or goodness when applied to them? Consistency would seem to require that those who brand the doctrine with so many hard names in the one case, should not shrink from the responsibility of characterizing it in the same way in the other also.

But there is still another fact to be presented, of no small weight in this discussion. Is it not sometimes overlooked, in the strong prejudice which is felt against this doctrine, that a very large portion of mankind do actually perish? Whether there be or be not such a thing as unconditional election to everlasting life—whether the doctrine be embraced or rejected—the *fact* is admitted by all, except Deists and Universalists, that multitudes of our race are lost eternally. We press this fact upon those who allege that our doctrine is a calumny upon the Deity. We call upon them to point out in what respect it is more derogatory to the Deity than *their own avowed belief* that many of the race are finally damned. We insist upon their showing that a single individual is lost, assuming our view of the doctrine of election, who would not be lost if the doctrine were expunged from the book of God's purposes. In other words, we require them to prove that election adds a solitary sinner to the number of them that perish. *We utterly deny that it does this.* We maintain that no man is made a sinner by this decree; and that no man will be condemned to hell for not being elected to salvation. That it is the non-elect who will be condemned, is most true; but the ground, the meritorious ground of their condemnation, will be, not the fact of their non-election, but the fact that they are sinners. Under the government of a righteous God, nothing but sin can be the ground of punishment: and non-election is no sin. The only fore-ordination of men to perdition, known to the Bible or to our Standards, is a fore-ordination of the wicked to wrath *on account of their sins*, not as some would represent, irrespective of their sins. The elect are chosen without any foresight of their faith or good works, solely by the good pleasure of the Almighty: the rest of the race are also contemplated by Him in their true moral character, that is, as sinners and rebels; and ON THE GROUND OF THEIR POSSESSING THIS CHARACTER, a character, let it be observed, which election has no agency in forming, they are "ordained to dishonor and wrath." In other words, the decree of election leaves the wicked where it found them. It is simply a "taking out" from among them, those who are chosen to eternal life; as we read, Acts xv. 14, in the speech of the apostle James at Jerusalem: "Simeon hath declared how God, at the first, did visit the Gentiles, to *take out of them* a people for his name." If none were thus "taken out," it is manifest, ALL would perish: so that election, as has been argued in the former part of this discourse, instead of increasing the number of the lost, lays the sole foundation for the salvation of any portion of the race.

Since, then, millions of the race are actually lost, and since the decree of election not only has no agency in the destruction of a single individual of this number, but secures the salvation of a multitude who would otherwise perish, we ask in what respect our doctrine is so derogatory to the Divine perfections; and we inquire of those who differ from us, how they will reconcile to His perfections, on their own principles, the perdition of so many of their fellow-creatures. Here are the two *facts*: God is infinitely upright, and wise, and good; and yet a large part of our race are to be shut up in hell for ever. How are these facts to be harmonized? If we are told that the perdition of the wicked does not impeach the divine goodness, because He would gladly save them *if he had the ability to do so*—that he has provided a Redeemer, instituted a system of means, and *done all that he could* to bring the whole race to repentance, but that in multitudes of cases he has failed of success, and his creatures have persevered in sin notwithstanding his utmost efforts to reclaim them,—if we are told this, we have, indeed, an answer to the question, and an adequate cause assigned for the destruction of the impenitent. But see what an answer! In order to vindicate the goodness of God, he is stripped of his power. The free-will of man is made paramount to the omnipotence of his Maker. Instead of that great and glorious Being who is clothed with majesty and strength, who "rideth upon the heavens," whose "voice is like the voice of many waters," who "hangeth the earth upon nothing," and "divideth the sea with his power," at whose reproof "the pillars of heaven tremble and are astonished," and before whom seraphs veil their faces: we have presented to us a Being, benevolent and amiable indeed, but utterly unable to govern his creatures, and who is obliged to stand by and see them perish in despite of every plan he can devise, and every influence he can employ to prevent it. Is *this* the God of the Bible? Is the Lord God Omnipotent really so imbecile a sovereign that his subjects can countervail his purposes and defeat plans which are identified with his own glory? And are we to be told by those who embrace these unworthy views of the Deity, that "the doctrine of election is derogatory to the divine character?" Does it befit *them* to rebuke the friends of this doctrine, who begin their vindication of the Almighty by breaking his sceptre, and taking off his crown, and pulling down the pillars of his throne, and proclaiming in the face of earth, and heaven, and hell, that the creatures he has formed out of the dust of his footstool, are independent of his control, and that he cannot save them unless in the exercise of their free-will they shall *permit* him to do it? We rejoice that we know no such divinity as this. Bad as our doctrine may be in the judgment of its opposers, it at least leaves us a GOD WHOM WE CAN RESPECT. Sooner than impugn the glorious majesty of the Godhead and degrade him to their standard, we would have "the clouds and darkness" which enwrap his throne, seven fold deeper, and the manifestations of his vengeance upon the vessels of wrath, seven fold more awful than they are. In reasoning upon his goodness we may err, especially when we are attempting, rather from the light of nature than from Scripture, to prescribe what his goodness may require him to do for an apostate race like our own. But we cannot err in ascribing to him absolute sovereignty over all the works of his hands.

We decline, then, the explanation on which others choose to rest, of the painful fact that millions of our race are actually lost. In our view, the fact assumed to explain it, viz.: that the Deity, though he desires to the utmost their salvation, has no ability to accomplish it, would involve, if established, an infinitely greater catastrophe to the universe, than the perdition of a thousand worlds like this. The only alternative which remains to us, is to fall back upon the Divine sovereignty. The all-wise God, for reasons unrevealed to us, has not seen fit to extend his pardoning mercy to the whole of the race, and a portion of them are left to suffer the just penalty of their sins. This solution may not be very flattering to our intellectual pride, nor very satisfactory to our curiosity; but it is the only one which the Scriptures furnish, and it must suffice us for the present life. I leave it to you to decide whether the difficulties with which the *fact* that so many perish is encumbered, are mitigated or eluded by discarding the doctrine of election; and whether this doctrine, fairly understood, contains anything so derogatory to the Deity, as the theories to which it stands opposed. The doctrine does indeed recognize his sovereignty, and herein it may disturb the composure of those who love to think of him only as the kind and compassionate Father of his creatures. But it is submitted to their candor, whether his paternal character is the only one in which the Scriptures present him to us. Let them turn, for example, to the first chapter of 1 Corinthians, where they will find it thus written:

> "For ye see your calling, brethren, how that not many wise men after the flesh, not many mighty, not many noble are called: but God hath chosen the foolish things of the world to confound the wise; and God hath chosen the weak things of the world to confound the things which are mighty; and base things of the world, and things which are despised, hath God chosen, yea, and things which are not, to bring to naught things that are: that no flesh should glory in his presence." —1 Cor. 1:26-29

And let them read the ninth chapter of Romans, and attend especially to this language:

> "I will have mercy on whom I will have mercy, and I will have compassion on whom I will have compassion. So then it is not of him that willeth, nor of him that runneth, but of God that showeth mercy...He hath mercy on whom he will have mercy, and whom he will he hardeneth." —Rom. 9:15-16

Can any impartial person fail to see that the Most High challenges to himself in these passages the loftiest prerogatives of a universal sovereignty? that He asserts his unqualified right to dispense his favors, and even to dispose of us, his rational creatures, after the counsel of his own will? Let the class of persons whom I now address, review again the *facts* which have been cited in this discussion,—the fall of our first parents, the endless diversity in the circumstances of mankind with respect to their spiritual privileges, the various calamities which overspread the earth, the apostasy and punishment of the angels, and the perdition of so many of our race,—and let them say whether these facts do not illustrate and confirm the testimony of Scripture, that God is as well a sovereign as a father. It avails nothing to avert our eyes from testimony like this. It is not to be neutralized by a refusal to consider it. And they who will consider it, cannot consistently object to the doctrine of election on the ground that it is derogatory to the Divine perfections, because they admit the existence of numerous *facts,* and, of course, believe them to be compatible with his perfections, which really involve the very exercise of sovereignty implied in this doctrine.

We agree with our brethren who reject the doctrine, that it is delightful to think of the incomprehensible and adorable Jehovah as our Father; and we have no higher joy than that which springs from the hope of being one day publicly owned by him as his children. But until every vestige of the flood is obliterated, and the Dead Sea has ceased to perpetuate the doom of Sodom and Gomorrah, and the lost angels are brought forth out of prison, and hell is annihilated, and the Bible is blotted out of existence, we cannot forget that he is also a righteous JUDGE and an almighty KING. Our sympathies prompt us to weep over the eternal destruction of so large a portion of our fellow-creatures; and we are ready to confess that we are utterly lost in attempting to explain the reasons why the race were permitted to fall, and why, having determined to give his beloved Son to retrieve the dreadful evils of the apostasy, the all-wise and merciful God was not pleased to extend the benefits of redemption to the whole human family. But our inability to unfold his secret purposes, furnishes us with no ground to cavil at his dispensations. Nor, unfathomable as the transaction is to our feeble faculties, are we able to detect in it aught that is "tyrannical" or "unjust." So far from it, we adore with gratitude unspeakable, the matchless love which, instead of suffering us *all* to perish, a procedure which would have left the justice of God untarnished, provided an atoning sacrifice of boundless worth, and brought up millions of the race from the confines of hell to the fruition of eternal blessedness. The character of Jehovah is not the less glorious in our eyes because in every part of this stupendous plan, we see it to be "glorious in holiness" as well as in mercy: nor is his throne the less attractive, because in the voice which proceeds from it, we find the MAJESTY OF A GOD blended with the tenderness of a FATHER.

THE DOCTRINE OF ELECTION NOT DISCOURAGING TO MAN

"Paul said to the centurion and the soldiers,
Except these abide in the ship, ye cannot be saved."
—Acts xxvii. 31

Of the two principal objections to the doctrine of election "one has immediate respect to God, the other to man. The former, which alleges that the doctrine is DEROGATORY TO GOD, has been considered: the latter, which affirms that it is DISCOURAGING TO MAN, I propose to examine now. This objection may be stated in the following form:—

"If the individuals to be saved have been selected, and their number unchangeably fixed by a divine decree, it must be useless for men to concern themselves about the question of their own salvation. If they are of the number of the elect, they will be saved whether they exert themselves to this end or not; if they are not, no efforts of their own can be of any avail. The omnipotent decree renders all human agency superfluous in the one case, and fruitless in the other. We have, therefore, but to fold our arms and await the issues to which we are severally appointed."

There are a number of points embraced in this objection, but they may be discussed collectively. I think it can be shown that it proceeds upon a serious misconception of the doctrine, and that no such consequences as are here specified, are fairly chargeable upon it. There are various lines of argument by which the difficulty might be met. I shall meet it by observing.

First, *That God has provided an atonement the value of which, in itself considered, is sufficient for the sins of all mankind.*

I speak not now of the purpose of God in respect to the application of redemption. The Scriptures do certainly teach, that Christ died as the substitute and surety of his own people, that is, of the people given him by the Father—that he "laid down his life for the sheep"—and that his blood shall be applied to all those included in the covenant of grace. But I speak of the intrinsic worth of his atonement, when I ascribe to it a value adequate to the redemption of all mankind. The proof of this lies in the fact that by reason of the union in his person of the divine and human natures, an infinite value must attach to his sufferings. A very few theologians adopting what has been styled the "Gethsemane view" of the atonement, have maintained that there was an exact commercial equivalency between his sufferings and the sins of his people, so that if there had been one more sinner to be redeemed, his sufferings must have been increased in a corresponding degree. But this scheme the great body of Calvinistic divines have rejected with abhorrence. They have concurred generally in the sentiment, that the sufferings of Christ would be sufficient, had it pleased the Father so to extend the benefits of redemption, to expiate the sins of every individual of our race.

I may be allowed to quote two eminent authorities on this subject. The first is Dr. Owen:

> "There is a sense in which Christ may be said to die for all and the whole world. His death was of sufficient dignity to have been made a ransom for all the sins of every one in the world; and on this, internal sufficiency is grounded the universality of the gospel offers."*

The other is the venerable Synod of Dort, which represented, two hundred years ago, the whole body of Calvinistic churches, (the church of England included:)

> "The death of the Son of God is a single and most perfect sacrifice and satisfaction for sins, of infinite value and price, abundantly sufficient to expiate the sins of the whole world."

And, again:

"Because many who are called by the gospel, do not repent nor believe in Christ, but perish in unbelief; this doth not arise from defect or insufficiency of the sacrifice offered by Christ, but from their own fault."

Secondly. *All men are authorized to avail themselves of the benefits of this atonement.*

They are offered indiscriminately to all. "Go ye into all the world, and preach the gospel to every creature." "Ho, every one that thirsteth, come ye to the waters." "Whosoever will, let him take of the water of life freely." "Look unto me, and be

---

* *Display of Arminianism*, ch. ix.
Articles of the Synod of Dort, ch. ii

ye saved, all the ends of the earth." Here is the warrant which every human being has to apply to Christ for salvation. And the warrant is the same to all, irrespective of character or condition. There is no restriction of the invitation to one part of the race; no exclusion of another part. The man who rejects it, has just as good a warrant for accepting as the man who does accept it. If confirmation of this were wanting, it might be found in the fact that the rejection of Christ is made a damning sin.

If Christ was not proposed to men as a Savior—if his atonement was not sufficient to expiate their sins "and they were not authorized to avail themselves of it, they could not be condemned for rejecting Him. But what saith the Scripture? "He that believeth and is baptized, shall be saved; he that believeth not, shall be damned." It is no sin to be of the number of the non-elect. We nowhere read of a sinner's being condemned for not having been chosen to eternal life. "*This* is the condemnation, that light is come into the world, and men loved darkness rather than light because their deeds were evil." The condemnation is that "when Christ calls, they refuse; when he stretches out his hands, they will not regard"— they "will not come to him that they may have life."

Thirdly. Even this is not all. God has not only provided a system of salvation of which all men are authorized and commanded to avail themselves; He has in many ways displayed his tender concern for their spiritual welfare. "As I live," he says, "I have no pleasure in the death of the wicked, but that the wicked turn from his way and live.

Turn ye, tum ye from your evil ways: for why will ye die?" To this solemn asseveration and appeal, he has added other most convincing evidences of his regard for our happiness. He has given us the Bible, the Sabbath, the preaching of the gospel, the ordinances of the sanctuary, the privilege of prayer, the ministrations of the Holy Spirit, the mercies and the chastisements of his providence, and by all these and other agencies he has hedged up, as it were, the way to destruction and made it impossible for men (in a Christian land) to perish, except they perish willfully. This whole array of means, supplied by his providence and grace, attests his paternal concern for his creatures, and leaves those who refuse to come to the marriage-supper of his Son, without the least excuse.

To these three propositions, which really cover the whole ground, the objector will probably answer as follows: "Allowing that the provision revealed in the gospel is sufficient in itself for the necessities of all men, and that all are authorized to embrace it; still, as a matter of fact, only the elect will embrace it, and unless we know ourselves to be of that number, we can have no motive to apply for it." On this I remark,—

1. That as the gospel proffers salvation to all men, and as it addresses them, not as elect or non-elect, but simply as sinners, *no sinner has any right to assume that he is not embraced in the divine purpose of mercy.* Whether he is or not, is a point which he can learn only from the result. To assume either the affirmative or negative of the question, is

to be guilty of criminal presumption. For what right has any creature to challenge to himself a knowledge of the secret purposes of God? And what greater infatuation can a man display than to regulate his conduct on the most important of all subjects, by a pretended knowledge of the divine decrees, or a random conjecture as to the allotment they assign to him? These decrees are not the rule of our duty. We are not held responsible for not conforming to them. We are not bound to act with the least reference to them, nor even to know what they are. So far from it, we cannot by all our searching find them out. "*Secret things belong unto God: those which are revealed belong to us and to our children.*" For complying with the written law, we are responsible. If we disobey or neglect that, it is at our peril. The word of God shows us at once our ruin and our remedy: condemns us as sinners, and offers us a Savior. With this, and this alone, we have to do. Why should we abandon a known for an unknown rule; the standard which God has placed in our hands, and on our conformity to which he has suspended our salvation, for a standard which our faculties can no more discover than they can comprehend the divine infinitude, and which God has nowhere required us to make the guide of our conduct?

2. Let it be particularly noted, that while the secret purposes of God are effectually concealed from us, *we are perfectly sure that there is nothing in the decree of election which forbids or prevents men from acceding to the terms of the gospel.*

There is a tone of remark sometimes indulged in on this

subject, which imports that God exerts a positive influence upon the minds of a portion of our race, to prevent their acceptance of the gospel offer. But this is certainly not the case. The contrary is apparent from what has been already stated respecting the atonement and the universal proclamation of mercy. It is a gross imputation upon the character of the Deity, to suppose that he would offer salvation to men and press it upon them in every form of argument and expostulation, and at the same time secretly restrain them from accepting it. It is not denied that He may withdraw his Spirit entirely from obdurate and impious sinners, and suffer them, as a punishment, to become still more hardened under the preaching of the gospel. Yet even in this case, as there is reason to believe, he does but leave them to themselves. The rejection of Christ is a sin; and to allege that the divine agency is efficiently put forth to constrain men to reject Christ, is to make God the author of sin. But "He cannot be tempted with evil, neither tempteth He any man." If men will not believe and repent—if they will not "come to Christ, that they may have life"—it is not a divine influence, but their own depravity which prevents. This is readily admitted by all who have been brought to repentance, as it would be also by those who are still in their sins, if they would (could) carefully examine their own hearts. The importance of this point will appear more clearly in connection with my next observation, viz.

3. *That the certainty of the result "to the eye of God "in respect to every individual of our race, compromises no one's freedom, and furnishes no ground for discouragement, and no excuse for unbelief.*

That the result is pre-determined in respect to every individual, may be proved both by reason and scripture. A God of infinite wisdom, goodness, power, and holiness, could not undertake to govern the universe without a plan; and no plan would be complete or exempt from liability to failure, which did not embrace the entire agency of every rational being. "Known unto God are all his works from the beginning of the world;" for "he worketh all things after the counsel of his own will." How these two things may consist together,—the sovereignty of God, working all things after the counsel of his own will,—and the freedom of man, is the great problem which has exercised the profoundest minds of every age, and which is still as far from being solved as ever. After pursuing the investigation to a certain point, we come to a chasm which the human intellect cannot bridge over. That illustrious metaphysician, Mr. Locke, expresses himself in the following modest and candid manner on this subject:—

> "If you will argue for or against liberty from consequences, I will not undertake to answer you. For I own freely to you the weakness of my understanding, that though it be unquestionable that there is omnipotence and omniscience in God, our Maker, and I cannot have a clearer perception of anything than that I am free, yet I cannot make freedom in man consistent with omnipotence and omniscience in God; though I am as fully persuaded of both, as of any truths I most firmly assent to. And therefore I have long since given off the consideration of that question, resolving all into this short conclusion, That if it be possible for God to make a free agent, then man is free, though I see not the way of it."

Our *Confession of Faith*, while asserting the doctrine of the divine decrees, rejects the consequences falsely charged upon that doctrine, one of which is, that it is incompatible with human liberty. "God, from all eternity, did by the most wise and holy counsel of his own will, freely and unchangeably ordain whatsoever comes to pass; yet so as thereby neither is God the author of sin, nor is violence offered to the will of the creatures, nor is the liberty or contingency of second causes taken away, but rather established." (Chap. iii. 1.) Our inability to harmonize the divine sovereignty and his fore-ordination of all things, with man's freedom, is no reason for rejecting either of these doctrines. We are not required to reconcile them; but since they are both propounded to us on adequate evidence, we are required to believe them (both). As regards our freedom, the appeal may be safely made to every man's consciousness. Freedom consists essentially in a power to will what, at the time and on the whole, appears to us best to be chosen. Is not every individual conscious that he possesses and is constantly exercising this power? The believer *wills* to take God as his portion, because this appears to him his wisest and best course. So he puts forth successive volitions to repent of his sins, to trust in Christ, to pray, to minister to the temporal or spiritual welfare of his fellow-creatures, to cast his contributions into the treasury of the Lord; because all these duties appear to him to be for the best—he *prefers* doing these things to anything else. He is conscious that he acts with perfect freedom. And this is the more observable, because we know from scripture that the agency of the Holy Spirit is concerned in the production of all holy volitions and gracious exercises. No less conscious is the unbeliever of acting freely in refusing to come to Christ.

He may, indeed, act counter to his deliberate judgment and his general convictions of duty, but he does what, at the time, he believes to be the best— he acts as he *chooses*—he "*does what he likes.*" You may listen to a sermon on the duty of immediate repentance. Your reason may be convinced, and your conscience may bid you obey the divine command: and yet you may, as you retire from the sanctuary, decide that you will not now repent, or, which is the same thing, that you will hold the subject under consideration for the present. You may listen here to one of our Savior's gracious invitations, and as his love and mercy are unveiled, and the glorious salvation he proffers you is described, you may be "*almost* persuaded to be a Christian;" and yet you may, on the whole, conclude that another season will answer better, and so continue in your sins. Now in these and all similar cases, you have the best possible evidence, the evidence of consciousness, that you are acting without constraint— you are doing what *you choose* to do. And this choice, as was proved under the last head, cannot be referred to any influence which God exerts upon you. *He* does not incline you to make these wrong decisions—decisions repeated every time you come to the sanctuary.

So far from it, he warns you against it. With mingled severity and tenderness, he expostulates with you, and bids you choose life and not death. It is not He who holds you back when you would follow the dictates of your judgment and conscience, but those corrupt, perverse appetites and passions which blind you to religion and chain you to the world. Nothing, therefore, could be more unreasonable than to fall back upon the unknown purposes of God, as a justification for continuing in sin; or to plead the fact that there are such purposes as a ground of discouragement in seeking your salvation. You have an irrefragable answer to all suggestions of this kind in your own breast; for you know that all you do, you do freely. That all your volitions should be comprised in God's plan, cannot affect your freedom; they are as free as though there were no such plan in existence.

And this leads to another observation on this topic. If, as we maintain, God exerts no efficient agency in producing the sinful volitions of men, then the objection under consideration lies as well against the doctrine of the divine foreknowledge as against the doctrine of decrees. The *certainty* of the result, it is alleged, makes all effort useless. Reserving a further answer to this difficulty until we come to the next head, I would observe here, that if we admit, as all Christians do, simply the foreknowledge of the Deity, we concede the pre-certainty of all events to Him. He must have known from eternity, who would under the renewing influences of his Spirit embrace the gospel, and who would reject it, and all the circumstances pertaining to each particular case. But how can this fact interfere with our liberty? How can it modify our conduct? How can it affect in any way our duties and responsibilities? If this foreknowledge was ours—if *we* were certain what was to be our future conduct with all its consequences—the case would be widely altered. But how can this certainty in God's mind influence us; or with what propriety can we appeal to it in deciding questions of duty?

There never was a battle fought, the issue of which was not as certain to God before as after it? Did this affect the plans or exertions of the hostile armies? The battle of New-Orleans took place a fortnight after the plenipotentiaries of the two powers had signed a treaty of peace. This fact was known not only to the Supreme Being, but to thousands of people in Europe. But did it have any influence upon the troops engaged in that contest? The awful disaster which overwhelmed one of our packet-ships near Liverpool a few months since, was certainly known to Omniscience before it occurred; but had his knowledge of it any influence upon the persons who embarked in that vessel? All that is to occur in Europe during the next six months, is known to God. He might, if he saw fit, reveal it to you. Would your knowledge of it, supposing you kept it to yourself, trench upon the liberty of a single individual there, or modify his conduct in the slightest degree? It seems almost puerile to multiply illustrations of this point. But men seem to ascribe I know not what mysterious and malign influence to the fact that their conduct is fore-known to God; and to imagine that they are on this ground less free than they would otherwise be in respect to their compliance with the terms of the gospel. I trust the fallacy of this impression has been made apparent to every reader: it will be still farther exposed as we proceed.

4. As the decree of election leaves the freedom of man unimpaired, *so it not only permits but requires the use of means in securing our salvation.*

"If I am to be saved, I shall be saved; if I am to be lost, I shall be lost. The issue is settled by a Divine decree, and my own exertions have nothing to do with it." This is a sentiment frequently uttered by men who are not disposed to give up their sins and make their peace with God. It is sometimes entertained also, by persons of a more serious turn, who really believe that the doctrine of election has interposed some new obstacle in the way of their salvation, and that it discountenances all effort on the part of the sinner.

This objection has already been answered. It has been shown that a sufficient provision has been made for the wants of the world—that all mankind are authorized and even commanded to avail themselves of it—and that God has manifested his concern for the spiritual welfare of our race, in the most unequivocal and affecting methods—that no individual has a right to assume that he is of the number of the non-elect, or to regulate his conduct in any particular by a pretended regard to the secret purposes of God—that there is nothing in the decree of election which forbids or prevents men from acceding to the terms of the gospel—and that the certainty of the result in every case, compromises no one's freedom, and furnishes neither any ground for discouragement, nor any excuse for unbelief. If these things are so, there can be no room whatever for the idea that the result must be all one, whether we exert ourselves to secure our salvation or not—a sentiment which is as much in conflict with the whole tenor of the Bible, as it is likely to be fatal to those who entertain it. To show that our doctrine is not open to this cavil, let it be noted.

That the Divine decrees embrace not only ends but means; and that both in temporal and spiritual things, where an end is decreed, the means by which it is to be reached or accomplished are also decreed.

I speak of "temporal" things here, because some persons appear to think that the Divine decrees are restricted to spiritual matters. This is so far from being a correct opinion, that the Scriptures represent *all* events, however trivial, as being embraced in those decrees. Reason teaches the same thing; for in the great concatenation of causes and effects, trifling and important events are so linked together, that the omission of the least link must have broken the whole chain. If the captive Israelites are to be emancipated, and a great commonwealth founded, the freest and the noblest the world had ever seen, an Egyptian princess, seeking her own recreation, must be brought down to the Nile, just at the place and at the time to rescue a Hebrew infant, cast upon the stream in an ark of bulrushes. If the downfall of Rome is to be averted, the decree which ensures it must no less include the cackling of the geese on the Capitoline Hill. If the American colonies are to become an independent and powerful Republic, the decree which ordains it must no less ordain that a colonial mother shall unwittingly reserve her beloved son to become the leader of their armies and the "Father of his country," by refusing her assent to his accepting a midshipman's warrant already obtained for him in the British Navy. Every harvest is included in the Divine purposes; but not the reaping without the sowing;—the issue of every voyage, but not the gain or loss, without the building and fitting out of the ship and all the skill and labour demanded by the enterprise. If it is decreed that you are to make an advantageous sale of goods, it is no less decreed that you are to go to your warehouse and show your customer the goods, and agree with him as to the terms. If it is decreed that you are to build yourself a house, it is equally decreed that you are, in person or by proxy, to purchase your lot and make the requisite contracts with the mechanics. If it is decreed that your children are to receive a good education, it is no less decreed that you are to employ suitable teachers. All this is readily admitted. It is only where the salvation of the soul is concerned, that men are chargeable with the folly and presumption of supposing that a Divine decree respecting the end, renders all use of means on their part nugatory. On this subject alone are they disposed to substitute the secret purposes of God for his revealed will (revealed whether in his word or by his providence,) as their rule of duty. On other subjects they obey the dictates of that common sense which was displayed by the companions of the apostle Paul in his shipwreck. After they had been driving about in the storm for "many days" he said to them, "There shall be no loss of any man's life among you, but of the ship. For there stood by me this night, the angel of God, whose I am and whom I serve, saying, Fear not, Paul, thou must be brought before Caesar; and lo, God hath given thee all them that sail with thee." (Acts xxvii. 22-24.) This was certainly, if the case could be, an assurance of preservation which would have warranted them in disregarding all means, and trusting solely to the Divine purpose for deliverance. But when, on the ship's striking, the apostle saw some of the sailors about getting into the boat to escape from the vessel, he said to the centurion and the soldiers, "Except these abide in the ship, ye cannot be saved." In other words, their deliverance was decreed; *but* it was decreed in connection *with the requisite means.* And believing this, the men did remain in the ship. Precisely in the same way, salvation is decreed, but the decree embraces in every instance the means by which it is to be accomplished. It is not the mere salvation of a sinner which is decreed, but *with* this, *all* the agencies which lead to it. The Divine purpose takes in his parentage, birth, residence, education, companions, business, successes, misfortunes, health, sicknesses, religious advantages , and all the influences by which his character and course of life are shaped and molded. Men, I repeat it, are not simply chosen to salvation; they are "chosen to salvation through sanctification of the Spirit and *belief of the truth.*" Faith and repentance are as much a part of the decree as salvation. God has given us his word, the Sabbath, the ministry, the privilege of prayer, and other blessings, as means of grace— as the appointed channels through which he ordinarily bestows salvation. These means must be used. The truth must be brought into contact with men's minds: it must be believed and obeyed. God had "much people" in Corinth. How did he save them? By sending Paul to preach to them. He had a people in Samaria, and Philip had to go and preach there. He had determined to save Cornelius and Peter was sent down to Cesarea to tell him and his household "all things that were commanded him of God." He had a people among us, and he sent them the gospel, and they gave heed to it and are saved. It was, indeed, decreed that they should give heed to it; but this they did not and could not know beforehand. They felt that it was their duty to do it, for the Divine command was too explicit to be mistaken; and, acting as freely as they had ever done in rejecting Christ, they "submitted themselves to the righteousness of God," and accepted his proffered mercy.

This is the duty of every individual who is yet out of Christ. There is not one of you that has not all the warrant and all the encouragement to repent and believe in Christ, which they had, prior to their conversion, who actually have repented and believed. It was not the unrevealed decrees of God on which they proceeded, but his written word. The same Savior invites *you* who invited them: the same God commands *you*; the same pardon is tendered *you*; the same heaven and hell are set before *you*. If you are blind, so were they. If you are impotent, so were they. If you are dead in trespasses and sins, so were they. But they called upon God for help, and so may you. They besought the Holy Spirit to give them light, and strength, and life—to deliver them from bondage, work repentance in their hearts, and lead them to Christ—*and so may you*. Do you allege that God heard their prayers, but you do not know that he would hear yours? They had no more assurance on this point, before they tried it, than you have—and this, by the way, is assurance enough. Do you urge that the Holy Spirit assisted them and did for them all they wanted? You have just as much ground to hope that he will assist you, as they had to expect his aid.— What, then, hinders your salvation? "*I do not know that I am elected.*" Do you know that you are to reach your house after this service, and do you mean to remain here until you have some assurance of it? Do you know whether this is to be a lucrative or a losing week in your business, and will you remain at home until you ascertain? Did you know, the last time you had a serious illness, whether you were to recover, and did you forego all means until it was revealed to you that you were to get well? Why should you use means to prolong your natural life, when the period of its duration is unalterably fixed? "His days are determined, the number of his months are with thee, thou hast appointed his bounds that he cannot pass." Why not say, when sick, "If I am to live, I shall live, whatever I leave undone; and if I am to die, I shall die, whatever I may do." The question of your salvation is not more irrevocably settled than is the term of your natural life; yet in this case you will neglect no means to preserve life; in that you will plead that there is a "decree," and refuse all means. Is this conduct defensible either at the bar of Scripture or reason?

What God has decreed concerning us we shall not know until we stand before him. But this we do know, that he offers us salvation, and commands all men every where to accept of it under penalty of eternal death, and that he exerts no influence upon us to prevent our complying with this requirement. Does it become us, in these circumstances, virtually to say to the Supreme Being that he has not done enough for our salvation?—That although He sent his only-begotten Son to die for us, and offers us an interest in his precious blood without money and without price, we will not receive him as our Savior unless He first places in our hands the Book of Life, and lets us turn over its leaves to see if our names are there? It might seem as though a bare possibility of escaping eternal misery and securing a place in heaven, would be sufficient to put every one upon the most earnest and untiring exertions—that nothing would be omitted which promised to contribute in the slightest degree to a result so vitally connected with our everlasting well-being. People who are in a burning house or a sinking ship, are not in the habit of waiting for a revelation from heaven to assure them that they shall not perish, but eagerly avail themselves of any expedients, even the most desperate, which may hold out the slightest hope of deliverance. It is only where the soul and eternity are concerned, that men would require God to put into their hands a title-deed to paradise as the condition on which they will *consent* to exert themselves for their own salvation—as though the Creator and not themselves were the obliged party in the case.

Individuals who in this way set both the Bible and common sense at defiance, and whose conduct in all secular transactions condemns their conduct on this subject, certainly have no reason to suppose that they are likely to be saved. God has authorized no man to expect salvation, who will not use the means of grace with all diligence and prayer. Salvation is bestowed freely; but it is not usually bestowed without being sought. If it is not worth seeking, it is not worth having. And for any man to allege that a divine decree has precluded him from seeking it, or that it is not offered him in the Bible in good faith, is simply untrue. If he will attend to what passes in his own mind when he is listening to the admonitions or invitations of the gospel, he will find that the influence which holds him back is an influence from within, not from above. Nor can he plead in answer to this "the want of ability to comply with the divine commands. This plea is both impertinent and irreverent, unless he has a sincere desire to obey those commands, and is actually endeavoring to comply with them as far as he can. That regeneration is the work of the Holy Spirit, and that "no man can come to Christ except the Father draw him" is most true. But there are some things which every man can do towards his own salvation, and which of course he is bound to do. He can as well employ his powers and faculties upon the subject of religion, as upon any other subject. He can study the scriptures as well as other books. He can pray. He can come to the sanctuary twice on the Sabbath "and spend the rest of the day in profitable reading, reflection, self-examination, and prayer. He can ordinarily attend lectures or prayer-meetings during the week; he can make conscience of putting off his sins; he can watch against his evil tempers; he can be more circumspect in his conduct, more faithful in the performance of his duties; he can avoid those scenes and associations which are most hostile to seriousness of mind, and seek those which will foster thoughtfulness, and strengthen him in turning from sin to holiness. All this, and more than this, he can do, and God requires it of him. "Search the scriptures." "Let the wicked forsake his way, and the unrighteous man his thoughts, and let him return to the Lord, who will have mercy upon him, and to our God, for he will abundantly pardon." "Ask, and ye shall receive; seek, and ye shall find; knock, and it shall be opened unto you." Now unless a man is doing these things, unless he is "striving to enter in at the strait gate," can he with any decency allege, as an excuse for his impenitence, that he has no ability to comply with God's commands? How or when does he expect to receive ability? *It is in the path of duty that God meets and helps his creatures.* "Work out your own salvation with fear and trembling, for it is God who worketh in you to will and to do of his good pleasure." It is the great incentive and encouragement we have to seek salvation, that in the humble and prayerful use of the means of grace we may expect to receive help from above. "Then shall ye know, if ye follow on to know the Lord." If we follow the light we have we shall have more. If we use the strength we have, it will be increased.

Sincere inquirers after the truth, who are disposed to do what has now been laid before you—who will forego all quibbling and excuse-making and take the word of God as their guide—so far from considering the doctrine of election as a ground of discouragement, should regard it as a source of hope and confidence. Indeed, this is the only proper light in which it can be viewed; for this doctrine alone lays a foundation for the salvation of any of our race; if none were chosen to eternal life, none would be saved. And those who are chosen, are ordinarily saved in the way or by the process just described. They are convinced of the truth of Christianity, and made to feel its importance: there springs up in their breasts a desire to "win Christ and be found in Him;" they are disposed to renounce the world, to "put away their sins by repentance and their iniquities by turning unto God;" they begin, therefore, to seek in earnest an interest in the Savior, by a conscientious and prayerful use of the means of grace, until they are at length enabled to receive and rest upon Christ as He is freely offered them in the gospel. In all this, from first to last, although they are conscious, and, from the nature of the human mind, can be conscious, only of their own exercises, they are under the gentle influences of the Holy Spirit. It was He who awakened their self-reproaches and their dissatisfaction with the world, who made them willing to renounce their sins, who disposed them to frequent the sanctuary, to read the Bible, and to address their importunate prayers to God, and who constrained them to come as helpless, polluted, lost sinners to that "fountain which has been opened for sin and for uncleanness." As to all, therefore, who are conscious of entertaining such sentiments as these—all who desire to be saved and who are disposed immediately to seek for salvation in *God's appointed way*—there is everything in the doctrine of election to animate and encourage them.

Those, however, who choose to employ themselves in cavilling at the truth—who are resolved to take the secret purposes of Jehovah instead of his revealed word, as their rule of duty, and to go on in their impenitence, heedless of all the love and mercy of the gospel—would do well to remember that God is as well a Sovereign as a Savior, and that He will in the end pour out His indignation "upon the vessels of wrath fitted to destruction." "He hath mercy on whom he will have mercy, and whom he will he hardeneth." Willful and obstinate sinners who refuse to believe the plain teachings of His Word, who virtually charge Him with injustice for not saving the whole race, and who even presume to plead His unrevealed decrees as an apology for their impiety, thus making the Holy One the "minister of sin," may be left to harden themselves in transgression until they make their perdition sure. If there be any of you who are treading on this dangerous ground, let me entreat you to fly from it while the door of mercy is yet open to you. Rest assured that if you perish, you will not have the poor consolation of charging your perdition either to the insufficiency of the atonement, or to the decree of predestination. You will then see that the mercy of God brought salvation to your very door, and that with the same right and the same encouragement to accept of it as any of your fellow-sinners, you thrust from you, and "*would* not come to Christ that you might have life." The consciousness that it was your own hand which barred the gates of heaven against you, will be the bitterest ingredient in your cup of misery: and of all the harrowing, heartrending sounds which will ring in your ears in that world of woe, the most agonizing and the most incessant will be that awful sentence, "THOU HAST DESTROYED THYSELF!"

Such is an imperfect exhibition of the Scripture doctrine of election, in respect to the two most popular and most serious objections to it. I trust it has been shown that this doctrine is not derogatory to the divine perfections; and that as regards man, it neither justifies a presumptuous self-confidence, nor is adapted to discourage the humble and conscientious inquirer after truth. Most of the difficulties and perplexities experienced on this subject, arise either from a misconception of the doctrine, or from that repugnance to the sovereignty of God which is a main element in our natural depravity. Whether the doctrine be true or not, is a question to be decided, not by our own feelings, nor by creeds and confessions, but by the Scriptures. Let me respectfully, but earnestly invite you, then, to examine your Bibles with diligence, honesty, and prayer, to ascertain "whether these things are so." And if you find that the doctrine of election is really taught in the word of God, let neither the arguments of the skeptical, the sneers of the ungodly, nor the ridicule of Christian professors who know too little of theology to wade even its shallowest brooks, prevent you from embracing and clinging to it.

> *"For all flesh is as grass, and all the glory of man as the flower of grass. The grass withereth, and the flower thereof falleth away: but* THE WORD OF THE LORD ENDURETH FOREVER. *And this is the Word, which by the gospel is preached unto you."*

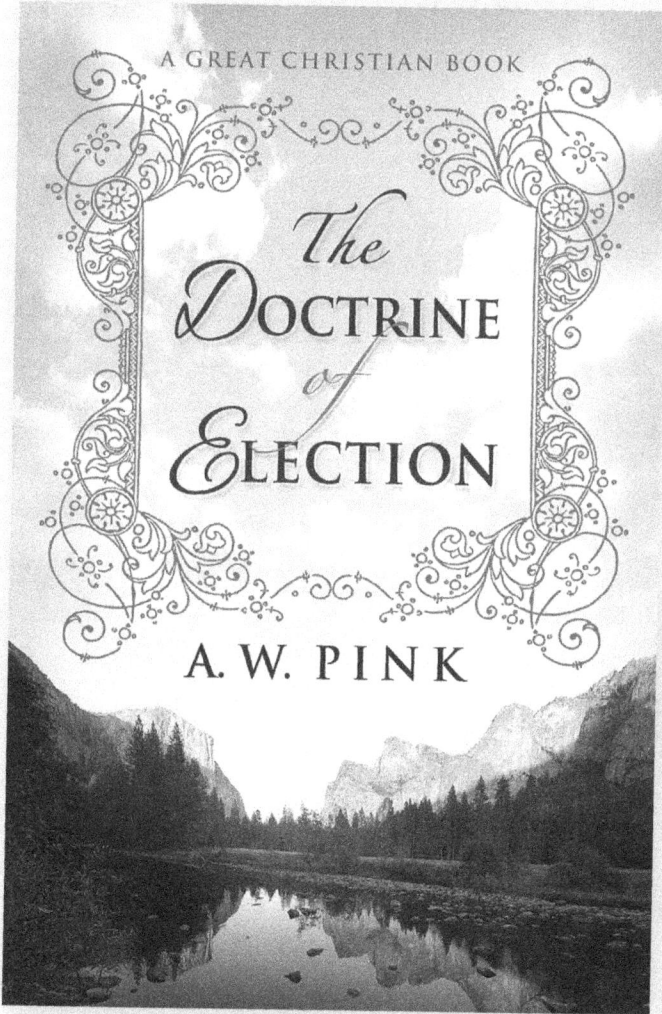

THE MISSION OF GREAT CHRISTIAN BOOKS

The ministry of Great Christian Books was established to glorify The Lord Jesus Christ and to be used by Him to expand and edify the kingdom of God while we occupy and anticipate Christ's glorious return. Great Christian Books will seek to accomplish this mission by publishing Gospel literature which is biblically faithful, relevant, and practically applicable to many of the serious spiritual needs of mankind upon the beginning of this new millennium. To do so we will always seek to boldly incorporate the truths of Scripture, especially those which were largely articulated as a body of theology during the Protestant Reformation of the sixteenth century and ensuing years. We gladly join our voice in the proclamations of— Scripture Alone, Faith Alone, Grace Alone, Christ Alone, and God's Glory Alone!

Our ministry seeks the blessing of our God as we seek His face to both confirm and support our labors for Him. Our prayers for this work can be summarized by two verses from the Book of Psalms:

"...let the beauty of the LORD our God be upon us, And establish the work of our hands for us; Yes, establish the work of our hands." —Psalm 90:17

"Not unto us, O LORD, not unto us, but to your name give glory." —Psalm 115:1

Great Christian Books appreciates the financial support of anyone who shares our burden and vision for publishing literature which combines sound Bible doctrine and practical exhortation in an age when too few so-called "Christian" publications do the same. We thank you in advance for any assistance you can give us in our labors to fulfill this important mission. May God bless you.

For a catalog of other great
Christian books including
additional titles on
the Doctrines of Grace—

contact us in
any of the following ways:

write us at:

Great Christian Books
160 37th Street
Lindenhurst, NY 11757

call us at:

(631) 956-0998

find us online:

www.greatchristianbooks.com

email us at:

mail@greatchristianbooks.com

www.ingramcontent.com/pod-product-compliance
Lightning Source LLC
Chambersburg PA
CBHW031633040426
42452CB00007B/816